MW01027577

Made in United States
North Haven, CT
08 December 2023

45329885R00074